**Grade 5**  Violin

# Improve your sight-reading!

## Paul Harris

**Extra Stage: Revision** available to download from
fabermusicstore.com

FABER *ff* MUSIC

# Practice chart

|  | Comments (from you, your teacher or parent) | Done! |
|---|---|---|
| Stage 1 |  |  |
| Stage 2 |  |  |
| Stage 3 |  |  |
| Stage 4 |  |  |
| Stage 5 |  |  |

Teacher's name _____

Telephone _____

With many thanks to Gillian Secret for her invaluable help.

© 2011 by Faber Music Ltd
This edition first published in 2011 by Faber Music Ltd.
Bloomsbury House 74–77 Great Russell Street London WC1B 3DA
Music processed by Donald Thomson
Cover and page design by Susan Clarke
Cover illustration by Drew Hillier
Printed in England by Caligraving Ltd

ISBN10: 0-571-53625-5
EAN13: 978-0-571-53625-2

US edition:
ISBN10: 0-571-53665-4
EAN13: 978-0-571-53665-8

To buy Faber Music publications or to find out about the full range of titles available
please contact your local music retailer or Faber Music sales enquiries:
Faber Music Ltd, Burnt Mill, Elizabeth Way, Harlow CM20 2HX
Tel: +44 (0) 1279 82 89 82   Fax: +44 (0) 1279 82 89 83
sales@fabermusic.com    fabermusicstore.com

# Introduction

Being a good sight-reader is so important and it's not difficult at all! If you work through this book carefully – always making sure that you really understand each exercise before you play it, you'll never have problems learning new pieces or doing well at sight-reading in exams!

## Using the workbook

### 1 Rhythmic exercises
Make sure you have grasped these fully before you go on to the melodic exercises: it is vital that you really know how the rhythms work. There are a number of ways to do the exercises – see *Improve your sight-reading* Grade 1 for more details.

### 2 Melodic exercises
These exercises use just the notes (and rhythms) for the Stage, and are organised into Sets which progress gradually. If you want to sight-read fluently and accurately, get into the simple habit of working through each exercise in the following ways before you begin to play it:
- Make sure you understand the rhythm and counting. Clap the exercise through.
- Know what notes you are going to play and the fingering you are going to use.
- Try to hear the piece through in your head. Always play the first note to help.

### 3 Prepared pieces
Work your way through the questions first, as these will help you to think about or 'prepare' the piece. Don't begin playing until you are pretty sure you know exactly how the piece goes.

### 4 Going solo!
It is now up to you to discover the clues in this series of practice pieces. Give yourself about a minute and do your best to understand the piece before you play. Check the rhythms and fingering, and try to hear the piece in your head.

Always remember to feel the pulse and to keep going steadily once you've begun. Good luck and happy sight-reading!

Terminology:
Bar = measure

# Stage 1

E major
A♭ major

## Rhythmic exercises

Remember to count at least two bars before you begin each exercise –
one out loud and one in your head.

## Melodic exercises

### Set 1: Exploring E major

**Set 2: Exploring A♭ major**

## Prepared pieces

> **1** What is the key of this piece? Play the scale and arpeggio in a range of dynamics from this piece.
>
> **2** Can you spot any repeated rhythmic patterns? Choose one of these patterns and improvise a short piece based on it.
>
> **3** Think through the fingering of the whole piece.
>
> **4** Tap the pulse and think the rhythm, then tap the rhythm and think the pulse.
>
> **5** How will you convey the character of the music?

Waltzing

> **1** In which key is this piece? Play the scale and arpeggio in the style of the piece.
>
> **2** Walk around the room to the pulse and sing the rhythm with gusto!
>
> **3** Think about the fingering, particularly where to shift.
>
> **4** Make up your own reel in the same key.
>
> **5** How will you put character into your performance?

With a hint of Killarny

# Going solo!

Don't forget to prepare each piece carefully before you play it.

# Stage 2

## Rhythmic exercises

Remember to count two bars before you begin each exercise –
one out loud and one in your head.

## Melodic exercises

### Set 1: Introducing dotted rhythms

Don't forget to count at least two bars in before
you begin the melodic exercises as well.

**Set 2: Adding more semiquavers**

# Prepared pieces

> 1 What is the key of this piece? Play the scale and arpeggio in the character of the piece.
>
> 2 Can you spot any repeated whole-bar patterns?
>
> 3 Think through your fingering: where will you shift?
>
> 4 Choose a pattern and improvise a short piece in a flowing style.
>
> 5 Play the first note and hear the piece through in your head.

**Flowing like a cool calm canal**

> 1 In which key is this piece? Play the scale with energy.
>
> 2 Study the first two bars for a few moments and then play them from memory.
>
> 3 Tap the pulse with your foot and the rhythm with your hands.
>
> 4 Think about how you will plan your bow speed through the piece.
>
> 5 How will you put character into your performance?

**With energy and excitement**

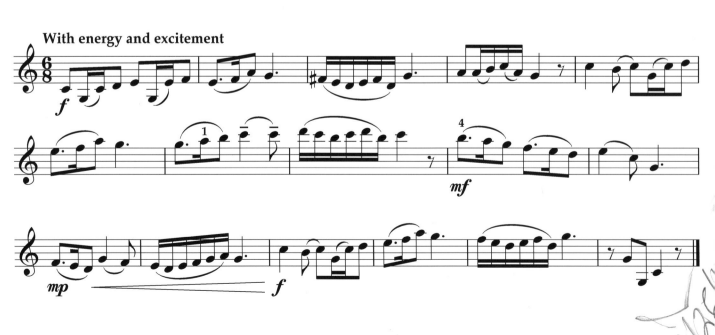

# Going solo!

Don't forget to prepare each piece carefully before you play it.

# Stage 3

B minor
C minor
More ties

## Rhythmic exercises

## Melodic exercises

### Set 1: Exploring B minor

## Set 2: Exploring C minor

## Prepared pieces

1 Play the scale and arpeggio softly and with a 'mesto' character.

2 To which pattern do the first three notes belong?

3 Tap the pulse strongly and think the rhythm, then tap the rhythm loudly and think the pulse.

4 Improvise slowly in this key. Make your improvisation long, and try to get lost in your music.

5 Play the first note and hear the piece through in your head, including dynamics.

1 In which key is this piece? Play the scale with a *cresc.* going up, and *dim.* coming down.

2 How many repeated ideas can you find?

3 Set a pulse going and hear the piece through in your head *at the same time*.

4 Study the first two bars for a few moments and then play them from memory.

5 How will you put character into your performance?

# Going solo! Don't forget to prepare each piece carefully before you play it.

# Stage 4

## Rhythmic exercises

Always count at least two bars before you begin each exercise
– one out loud and one silently.

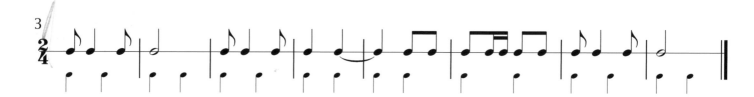

## Melodic exercises

### Set 1: Introducing syncopation
What do you notice about the next two exercises?

## Set 2: Exploring syncopation and pizzicato

# Prepared pieces

1 Play the scale of this piece with a *crescendo* ascending, and *diminuendo* descending, and a *rall.* at the end.

2 Think through the bowing of the piece, and in particular the bow speed.

3 What will you count? Tap the pulse strongly and think the rhythm, then tap the rhythm strongly and think the pulse.

4 What is the music's character? How will you convey this?

5 Play the first note and hear the piece through in your head, including musical expression.

1 In which key is this piece? Play the scale cheerfully.

2 How many repeated ideas can you find?

3 Tap the pulse with your left hand and the rhythm in your right. Then repeat the other way around.

4 Study the first two bars for a few moments, then play them from memory.

5 Play the first note and then hear the piece through in your head.

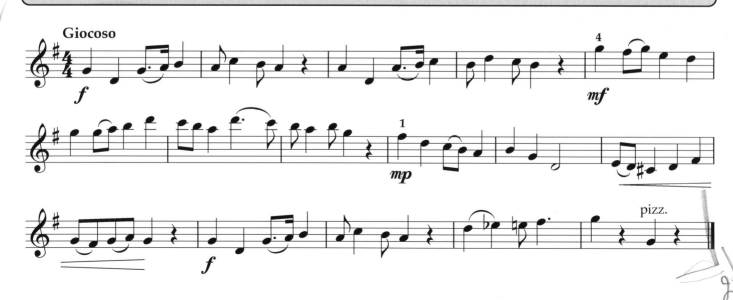

# Going solo!

Don't forget to prepare each piece carefully before you play it.

# Stage 5

## Rhythmic exercises

## Perfect preparation

Here is the ideal way to prepare a piece of sight reading.
Get into the habit of working through this four-point plan before
you play each piece:

**1** Scan the whole piece, getting a feel for the meaning. Think
about the character by noticing the clues: tempo marking,
dynamic levels, rhythm and other markings.

**2** Look for passages where you might have to shift or take care
over bow speed.

**3** Try to hear the piece in your head. Don't worry about the pitch
being accurate – just aim to get a good overall idea of the piece.

**4** Decide on a pulse and count in two bars before you begin.

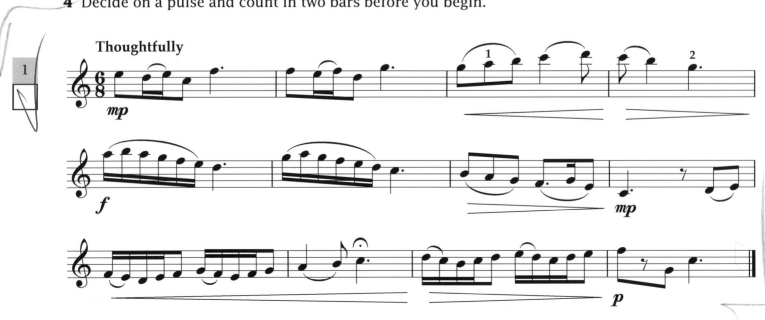

# Prepared pieces

> 1 Play the scale of C minor using some of the marked dynamics.
>
> 2 Why is this piece easier than it looks at first?
>
> 3 How many bars don't contain scale shapes?
>
> 4 What will you count? Tap the pulse strongly and think the rhythm, then tap
>   the rhythm softly and think the pulse.
>
> 5 Play a C and imagine playing the piece through confidently.

> 1 In which key is this piece? Play the scale like a dance.
>
> 2 Do any bars have the same rhythm?
>
> 3 Think the pulse and tap the rhythm backwards, beginning at the end!
>
> 4 Study any two bars for a few moments, and then play them from memory.
>
> 5 Play the first note and then hear the piece through in your head.

# Going solo!

Don't forget to prepare each piece carefully before you play it.

# The golden rules

**A sight-reading checklist**

Before you begin to play a piece at sight, always consider the following:

1 Look at the piece for about half a minute and try to feel that you are *understanding* what you see (just like reading these words).

2 Look at the time signature and decide how you will count the piece.

3 Look at the key signature and think about how to finger the notes.

4 Notice patterns – especially those that repeat, or are based on scales and arpeggios.

5 Notice any markings that will help you convey the character.

6 Don't begin until you think you are going to play the piece accurately.

7 Count at least one bar in.

**When performing a sight-reading piece**

1 Keep feeling the pulse.

2 Keep going at a steady tempo.

3 Remember the finger pattern of the key you are in.

4 Ignore mistakes.

5 Look ahead – at least to the next note.

6 Play musically, always trying to convey the character of the music.